Dreams from a Black Nebula

Dreams from a Black Nebula

Wade German

Hippocampus Press

New York

Frontispiece photograph: Rho Ophiuchi nebula © 2012 by Jack Newton.
Cover artwork "Artefact" copyright © 2014 by Dariusz Zawadzki. Image
courtesy of Morpheus Fine Art.

Acknowledgments: see p. 133.

Published by Hippocampus Press
P.O. Box 641, New York, NY 10156.
http://www.hippocampuspress.com

Cover design by Barbara Briggs Silbert.
Hippocampus Press logo designed by Anastasia Damianakos.

First Edition
1 3 5 7 9 8 6 4 2

ISBN13: 978-1-61498-102-2

CONTENTS

PHANTASMAGORICAL REALMS

Starry Wisdom

The darkness brings the cryptic stars
With outer mysteries to tell;
And to my mind, their myriads are
Like flowers of the outer hells
As night has brought the cryptic stars.

The darkness brings the cryptic stars,
And demons stir their sable wings
As night-winds rise from realms afar
To augur eldritch happenings
As night has brought the cryptic stars.

The darkness brings the cryptic stars,
And I would seek to be ordained
By all their astral avatars—
I hear their whisperings arcane
As night has brought the cryptic stars.

New Lost Worlds

The midnight moons ascend their ebon thrones
Above the monstrous ruins on the sand
Of this new desert world, named Samarkand,
Where hollow night-winds sentiently moan
Like voices calling on old sorceries
By subtle incantation of strange runes,
And weave fantastic weird among the dunes,
Conjuring phantoms of antiquity.

The city stands as it once did before:
Strong incense burns on altars in great fanes
Of alien gods, whose idols seem in pain,
As if omniscient of the coming wars
That swept away their priests and acolytes,
Whose shadows now perform their ancient rites.

The Black Idol

In ancient scrolls of astronomic lore,
The off-world seers wrote a god would fly
Earthwards, plummeting through the fathomed skies—
This monolithic block of jet black ore.
For eons it has ebbed an effluence
Of immemorial evil; lured primal men
To carve an image on the block, and then
Bow before its alien influence.

Now only wizard covens here converse.
They wield their spells like keys to open ways,
And they invoke the idol's avatars—
Conjuring from across the universe
The hordes that gather in dark nebulae,
The shapeless shadow from beyond the stars.

The Witch of Time

She came to me from some far otherwhere
Amid the dusky witchery of dawn,
The hour when my reveries had gone
To roam in alien, exotic airs.
She kissed me, and her philtred spell was cast:
The voices of old kingdoms I could hear;
And as a vizier and prophetic seer
My visions walked in temples of the past.

And through the swirling mists of bygone years,
Ascending stairs of muted centuries,
The elder demigods and deities
Strode forth upon the shrines of holy fear
To take their sacrificial feast of screams . . .
The witch's poison laughter broke my dream.

The Black Abbess

I died ten thousand years ago . . . then woke
In catacombs beneath the priory;
Then raised my sisters sleeping near to me
By whispered necromancies that I spoke;
And now the chapel fills with censer smoke
As I resume my ancient ministry—
And in black rites of outer mystery
The names of patron demons I invoke.

Shadows obey me; lich and mummy show
Allegiance to my long-forgotten sect.
Like moths ensorcelled by the moon's green gloom,
My spectral envoys flit among the tombs
To whisper gospel, and I resurrect
The dreams of gods sepulchered long ago.

The Demon Sea

Its shoreline borders on the edge of Time
Where demon-throated winds eternally moan
Across red sands and jutting, giant bones
Of alien sea-things, wreathed by weeds and slime.
Out in the gulf, huge shadows flit below
The raving waves in ever-shifting tides
Ensorcelled by the seven moons, which glide
Like ghosts above the sea's vermilion glow.

And in the churning chaos of the waves,
Vast hulks of vessels built by unknown race
Seem ruined castles and necropoli,
Where bloated devils like black octopi
Breed eldritch, evil dreams among the graves
Of mariners once lured here through deep space.

Astral Hierarchy

At twilight comes the minor moon
To float in skies of purple wine,
And desert spirits walk attuned
To subtle prodigies and signs
Beneath the glowing minor moon.

Then rising is the second moon—
It looms behind the minor sphere,
And night is litten as at noon
Awhile, as midnight's atmosphere
Lies mute beneath the second moon.

Then over all, the major moon
Arises like a queen of Hell;
Weird crimson light illumes the dunes,
And all seems in a wizard spell
Beneath the glowing major moon.

In Ultima Thule

In dreams beyond the borders of the known
I saw emerging cliffs like tattered ghosts,
Then harbored on the mist-enveloped coast
And followed through the woods a path of stones.
My memories had walked here once before—
The inner sanctum of the eldritch trees,
Where shadows woven of old warlockries
Reached out and whispered time-enshrouded lore.

And here were ruins of an elder race—
The relics of druidic cults of Mu,
Whose witches in their ancient wisdom knew
The language of the spirits of this place;
They traveled here, and marked the stones with runes
So others might with daemons here commune.

December in the Druid Woods

The moon casts down a corpse-white radiance
Upon the grove of ancient wizard oaks,
Where through the rows, an icy wind invokes
An evensong to unknown eminence.
Gnarled limbs now animate in eerie light;
They hail a presence in their somber rows,
Their shadows flattened on the glowing snow,
As if obeisant to the very night.

The wood is like a hidden world revealed,
A portal on its own primeval past—
Through which a spirit, since those times concealed,
Now moves namelessly, ineffable and vast;
Supernal in its cold nocturnal grace
And silent as the starry vault of space.

Château Nevreant

The cypress shadows spread a cryptic gloom
Across the portal of the old château;
And statues in the courtyard weirdly loom
Like watchers on an alien plateau.
Past crumbling stairs, dark halls and chambers seem
Too vast and void of solace for repose—
As if supernal forces had enclosed
This space in strange dimensions of a dream.

Dark echoes out of time are anchored here.
The portraits, armor, faded tapestries
Would speak of baleful crimes and unknown things;
As if a word might summon to appear
The presence of a spectral agency
Still bound by spells in some conjurer's ring.

Swamp Fantasy

Beyond the low black hills the bloodmoon sets.
Across the swamp, pale crimson light recedes
As from the darkness blacker shadows bleed,
Enfolding buzzing hummock, pond in jet.
Strange glowing mists, like spectral limbs, arise
And slither through the black rank grass and reeds,
The putrid flowers from the demon seeds
That drifted here from dark star-haunted skies.

Alone and exiled here a gray witch dwells:
Her dreams and visions, by swamp vapors fed,
Flow forth from wellsprings where she draws weird spells
By which she speaks to spirits of the dead
While shapeless things among the sedges lurk,
Conjured from out the swampland cauldron murk.

Valley of the Sorcerers

Once lush and green, the valley lies long dead—
A crimson canyon of which legend speaks:
Where witch-cults in their legions came to seek
Black lotus bloom for visions that it fed;
And white cacti, for rites in which conjured
Weird apparitions from the astral planes—
And shadows of those rituals remain
In spectral shapes which roam the cliffs unheard.

Strange relics in the valley have been found:
Black amulets and bone-carved talismans—
But some say that their owners meet strange dooms;
And elders of the nearest desert clans
Speak how defilers of the wizard grounds
Have lost their souls within the mummy tombs.

Moonflowers

The moon is like a demon's tomb,
A symbol of some ancient creed;
And by its gleaming, weird and white,
The lunar flowers are in bloom,
And in the shadows, seem to feed
Upon the essence of the night.

And as they bloom, the muted air
Transmutes as if by alchemy—
A warm elixir floods the zone
And hovers like a phantom there;
It haunts me like a reverie
In aspect other and unknown.

Then in the perfume's perfect spell,
I see the garden for a shrine:
The flowers—faces of pale nuns,
Whose fang-tipped lips and scent compel
New votaries into the vines
To meet with strange oblivion.

Hendecasyllabics

(After Swinburne)

In the month of the seventh moon of Saturn,
I, surveying the landscape spread before me,
Placed my feet on a path and outward wandered
Dead dry land in the realm beyond the border,
Crossing region of rock and giant craters
Till I reached in the twilight open desert—
Strange red reaches of dune and desolation
Endless, emptied of all, without oases,
Where I saw the mirages merge with shadows,
Flitting spectrally out among the ruins
Half submerged in the sand—the ancient temples.
Twilight faded and turned to early evening;
Flowing eerily, silent strange auroras
Spread green veils as of fire on the heavens.
Fearing horrors that hunt the outer spaces,
I then entered the dead and dreamlike city;
Built by giants it seemed, by size of portals,
Huge stone steps, of a Titan race forgotten.
Here I sheltered among a row of idols,
Dead gods looming on every side around me;
Sad strange faces before their silent altars,

Dreams from a Black Nebula

Weeping statues of gods unknown and nameless.
Sleeping there in a shadowed corner alcove,
I arose to the smell of sickly incense,
Strong sweet scent from the oils of evil flowers;
And I heard as an echo, sound of voices
In Old Speech, as I thought (a tongue I knew not):
Odd monotonous droning, near hypnotic,
That I took for the sound of fervent prayers,
Song or scripture of elder holy prophets.
Searching after its source, I found the figures
Up dark steps in a dim-lit vaulted chamber—
Darkly robed, with their hooded faces hidden,
Standing ominous, chanting verse in chorus,
Vocals echoing outer spheres of chaos.
All my spirit was shaken out of slumber,
And I saw, as it were, a revelation:
Deeper darkness amid the darkness gathered
Cloud-like, billowing forth a living shadow,
Cold and shining in black apotheosis,
Full of eyes as of glowing crimson embers . . .
Then I stirred to the sighs of swirling whirlwinds
Weirdly circling the sand in ghostly gyrings;
League on league by the moonlit waste surrounded,
I saw not any sign of ruined temples,
But beheld in the heavens high above me
Shadows moving across the stars and planets.

Walpurgisnacht

Past moondawn in primeval woods
The trees are pillars of a shrine;
And shadows, like some darkling brood,
Seem ministers who intertwine
With congregants all gathered on this night
Attendant to an awful, ancient rite.

The moon shines through a gauzy veil
Like superstition on the place—
Where moans and metaphysic wails,
Like echoes out of time and space,
Arise while witch and demon interbreed
And things emerge from black Sabbatic seeds.

Spectral Province

The fog is like a prophet's shroud,
A mystic whiteness, which obscures
The features of the realm in cloud;
And in the city, nothing stirs;
Its utter stillness makes all seem
Embalmed in outer dark of dreams.

Vague shadows in the mist appear;
My query passes through the veil
To formless shapes that shuffle near;
They pass, they pass, so gaunt and pale,
As quiet as the dead are mute . . .
Deep silence reigns here, absolute.

HYPNAGOGIC TERRAIN

Beyond the Wall of Tsang

Beyond the mountains, leagues of iron land
Reach out remotely, endlessly; then on
To arid ash-gray steppes where few had gone
En route to other regions, without plan
To find what they found there. Returned insane,
They whispered of converged realities—
And corpses eaten by the devotees
At crude stone temples on the dead gray plain.

Since then no caravan has traveled there.
But stranger pilgrims still would seek to know
Of wisdom hidden on that high plateau,
So dare its solitudes of cold thin air
To find those temples and their ghoul-faced priests,
The sacred mysteries of charnel feast.

A Voyage to Carcosa

(After *The King in Yellow* by Robert W. Chambers)

She closed the book that bears a cryptic sign
And drifted though a wall of purple cloud,
Her reason woven in a yellow shroud
And mummified within a shriven mind—

She saw the city's silhouette by moon;
Then walked Carcosa's whisper-stained dead streets
Expectantly (as fools their fate would greet),
Her thoughts like shadows lengthening at noon
That reached unto unhallowed Hali's shores
And blended with black mists of ecstasy,
The lake reflecting unknown stellar seas
While strains of madness threaded through the nerve
Of night's vast dynasty—

she stood before
The hidden king whom emperors have served.

In Carsultyal

(For the shade of Karl Edward Wagner)

I cross the threshold of a lucid dream
To primal lands, where crimson twilight fades
On lost Carsultyal. Evening shadows teem;
And all the darkness weaves with many shades
Around this ruined city of basalt
Where pacts of eldritch sorcery were made
And wizards forged black demon-hearted blades
That thirsted at vile altars in deep vaults.

The night winds rise, and shrieking eerily,
Phantasmal things that hail from other planes
Descend on silent shrines, deserted fanes;
While rising like a bloody scimitar,
The devil moon gleams ancient sorcery
In black skies swarming with their spawn of stars.

The House of Neptune

Submerged in deep blue fathoms like a dream,
The remnants of a mansion lie outspread
In crypt-like splendor on the ocean bed.
Dim sunlight falls in mute refracted beams
On spires, domes, and toppled colonnades
In gardens of blue kelp and amber weeds,
Where men and merfolk once exchanged their creeds
In temples hewn from emerald and jade.

Around the cryptic house of sunken stone,
The ruined arches, gates, and shadowed doors
Bear glyphs and symbols of forgotten lore,
Which ring an elemental sorcery
Around a green finned demon, crowned and throned,
Who dreams the ancient secrets of the seas.

Restoration

Since birth I've known that runes of sorcery
Were written in my blood by elder kin;
I hear them calling from the world within,
From dark eroded tombs of memory.
Their patron demon's spirit moves through me,
Like water rising deep beneath my skin;
Its rippling voice is near but ghostly thin,
And whispers through the snowy hills and trees.

A new age dawns; I feel the pale sun's rays.
In rising mists are specters of old myths.
I walk through rows of mossy megaliths
Where witch and warlock once enshrined our ways
With elementals of the sky and streams . . .
And ghosts of gods awaken from old dreams.

The Night Forest

I saw the shadows moving there
Like sentinels among the trees;
They stood like symbols in the air
Of long-forgotten memory.

Like sentinels among the trees,
Arisen from the ancient night
Of long-forgotten memory,
They gathered in the pale moonlight.

Arisen out of ancient night,
As if attendant to old ways,
They gathered in the pale moonlight,
Arisen out of other days.

As if attendant to old ways,
They stood like symbols in the air
Arisen out of other days—
I knew the shadows moving there.

Shadow and Silence

—After Poe

A demon spoke to me a rune:
Strange things in time shall be unsealed
Beneath a sky without a moon,
And secret things shall be revealed.

Strange things in time shall be unsealed
Without a shadow of a sound;
And secret things shall be revealed
In silence on a shadowed ground.

Without a shadow of a sound,
An ebon sleep as smooth as glass
Like silence on a shadowed ground
For many centuries shall pass.

An ebon sleep as smooth as glass
Beneath a sky without a moon
For many centuries shall pass.
And thus the demon spoke his rune.

Prophecy of the Red Death

From lower space where stars and planets dream,
A bloodstone moon within the heavens rose
And weirdly lit the night upon a world
In winter's crystal heart and cold white hold.
And every living creature stirred in sleep
When all the whiteness of their world went red.

Strange shadows crept in every shade of red
And colored every dreamer's living dream
With scarlet stains that splashed the walls of sleep.
And every dreamer from red horror rose,
Awakened by bright wonder, to behold
A blood-red snow had shrouded all the world.

Through crimson mist the sun rose on the world
As all God's children wondered at the red.
And they believed themselves in nightmare's hold,
That all now shared in some collective dream—
That they had passed from dream to dream, then rose
To walk in seasons of another sleep.

But they knew not their sleep was not a sleep
As ruby raindrops rained upon a world
Where all the living leaves were reddest rose
And rivers ran in rippling veins of red

And carmine lakes lay mute in placid dreams
Through all the months that spring and summer hold.

The hale held heart, but faith they failed to hold
As autumn came with awful fever sleep,
From which there flowered fearful evil dreams
In every region of a fearing world
Where hills and valleys bloomed with burden red,
Vermilion amaranth, and violent rose.

And then the sanguine sun no longer rose—
Now each and every soul sought hands to hold
As every face was febrile, flushed with red
And recognition: *death is but a sleep*–
And sleep fell fast upon a dreaming world
Where death held strange dominion over dreams.

And thus the moon rose on a house of sleep
Like some great bloodstone—risen to hold the world
In deep red shadows of eternal dream.

Lemurian Night Dive

Lost temples far beneath the waves
And vaulted, vast necropoli—
These phosphorescent coral caves
Seem temples far beneath the waves;
All weirdly hieroglyph-engraved
Like alien sarcophagi,
These temples far beneath the waves,
These vaulted, vast necropoli.

Oneiromancy

My dream was perfect as a sphere
On which a wizard set his gaze
To scry the misted atmosphere:
My dream as perfect as a sphere—
A crystal, in which ghosts appeared,
Who by an invocation raised
My dream: perfect as a sphere,
On which the wizard set his gaze.

Grimoire

This flesh-bound volume is a door;
And all its crimson glyphs recall
Lost chronicles of elder lore,
Written by primal minds before
The human worm had learned to crawl.

Each crumbling page is like a stair,
By which I climb the outer deeps
Through vaults of time and evil air,
Where dwellers sleep in crypt-like lairs
Beneath remote, occulted keeps;

And there I call on dreaming things
Outside dimensions of our own;
And to my song of summoning
They speak of ancient worshipping
And knowledge by my kind unknown.

I give them vows; they grant me keys—
I shall unlock the gate, and turn
Towards dark space and temporal seas . . .
And master alien alchemies
For which my ancestors were burned.

The Necromantic Wine

Where wattled monsters redly gape, that guard
A cowled magician peering on the damned
Through vials in which a splendid poison burns.

—George Sterling

In simultaneous ruin, all my dreams
Fall like a rack of fuming vapors raised
To semblance by a necromant, and leave
Spirit and sense unthinkably alone
Above a universe of shrouded stars.

—Clark Ashton Smith

The blood-red sun begins its slow descent
Behind the distant, jagged line of peaks.
From this clear vantage on the flagstone roof
Where I have made a final hermitage
Of this abandoned tower in deep woods,
I watch those giant, granite faces turn
From shades of gray to shade of cobalt blue;
And there above them, gliding on great wings,
I see the silver dragons in their flight
Returning to their eyries and high keeps.
The cool autumnal winds around me gust,
And now about me whirls a weirder breeze

Which whispers in my ear a rhyming rune—
And so an elemental speaks to me
Of her day's wanderings across the world,
And up into our planet's airless zones
That limited her flight to view the stars
Behind the vault of deep cerulean.
And now the wind grows wilder; she departs
To seek ethereal games with her own kind,
Amongst the changeling colors of the clouds
Aflame in twilight's final renderings.
The air grows cooler; so I step inside
And settle in beside the flame-fed hearth
To warm my bones, and smoke my briar pipe;
And lounging in narcotic quietude
I sip pale yellow wine and contemplate
The subtle incantations of the night.

But mortal issues rise to cloud my thought,
The same gray ghost that lately haunts the nights
Of this, my ancient age by sorcery
Sustained so many years beyond its span:
It seems I have grown weary of the world.
In youth, pursuit of wisdom was my quest,
And wonder, that bright star, had served as guide;
But somewhere in the passing centuries
Its brilliant fire dwindled; nearly dead,
That fulgent glow of wonder has gone out.
With what to stir the embers just a bit?
Despite the learning of three hundred years,

I never have held counsel with the dead;
I have but theories anyone might have
Of death's dimension and what lies beyond.
Ancestral imprecations on black arts
Have kept my line from straying to that gate;
But lately, I have pondered that old pact,
For there are other ways to gain the roads
Which dark magicians tread to seek strange truths;
I need not raise a corpse from its repose
By crude reanimation, or invoke
The wraiths who linger at unquiet graves;
I need not deal with ghouls in catacombs
Who sup on foul corruption in the crypt,
Nor need I bow to idols of dark gods.
Such methods—so impious and perverse!
There is a rarer magic, more refined
And suited to an acolyte of taste
Who would not risk an old familial curse . . .

I once discovered in a desert tomb
Strange hieroglyphs engraved upon a stone
That mentioned of a necromantic wine:
A darkling, ruby wine of philtered spells
Distilled in huge alembics of a dream
A demigod once dreamt who, dying, spilled
The poison in a glass canopic jar
Attendant demons slew each other for.
Another mention of the wine is here,
In this Lemurian scroll: it is described

As wine both sweet and bitter to the tongue,
With mystic operations on the mind
Inscribing arcane words of alchemy.
In one grimoire, the potion is compared
To green absinthe—pale opalescent drops
Evolving in the poet-prophet's brow
A third eye blazing like a demon star
That sees behind occulted nature's veil.
And one old libram notes the legend well,
But states the ruby potion is composed
Of substances abused by oracles:
The pollen of black loti thrice refined
And alkaloids from flowers of the moon,
Affording hypnagogic properties
On those who seek to see the dead in dreams.
And such I know of necromantic wine.
Who knows for sure what wisdom it imparts?
I have a bottle here; there is one thing
Betwixt this rare elixir's spell and me:
The cork.

      A darkness washes over me
Mere moments after sipping from the glass.
I shudder as a mist invades my mind,
The potion working like an anodyne.
My pulse throbs slowly, thudding as in sleep;
A sense of distance gathers in my head:
The chamber walls and ceiling now withdraw,
And all the candles glimmer distantly

Like witchlights in a black expanding pool.
I feel my body sink into the couch
And feel its fabric fray and then dissolve;
My atoms scatter as a thing destroyed.
Thus disembodied, and by wraith winds borne,
I am conveyed across the gulfs of night
And outer voids of undimensioned space
As swift hallucinations pass me by,
Successive strange horizons which unfold
Like tapestries, their imagery arrayed
In vast prismatic patterns which reveal
The surfaces of endless unknown worlds:
Strange vales and vistas, alien terrenes
With protean shores awash in pulsing hues,
The spans of all their suns and pendant moons.
But now the swarming throng of orbs disperse
And vanish out beyond my vision's reach
To merge with infinite immensities.
Now, in a region of black space, I see
A planet out of chaos newly formed:
Enormous storms that feed electric bale
Sweep red primordial skies with raving winds
As climates alternate in swift extremes.
Below the raging upper atmosphere,
Volcanoes bleed with endless lava flows,
And crimson rivers web a rifted main
Which quakes in primal night devoid of life.
And as the orb around its sun revolves,

Its smoking cauldron surface stills and cools,
And on it protoplasmic ichor gels:
Amoebic life-forms mindlessly evolve
And multiply at blind malignant rate—
The ancestors that spawn a fledgling race
Which treads across the dawns of centuries—
I see the rise of empires in time
And just as swiftly, witness their declines
By mode of nature or by work of man—
The cities lie collapsed in sunken seas
Or buried in abyssals of black sand;
The landscape quickly molders and decays;
The orb is now a planetary tomb
Where only subtle shadows faintly flit
Among the shrines and toppled monuments.
Again the vision fades. All sense deranged,
I hurtle through the interstellar deeps
And pass through regions of galactic cloud
Where I behold vast nurseries of stars
Which gleam like hellish rubies, xanthics, pearls
And fire opals blazing into birth;
Then further, on accelerated course
Through unlit oceans of the outer dark
Until my flight decelerates in zones
Where Time's great gears have shuddered to a halt.
I stand upon the rim of the unknown.
Below me swirls a strange, phantasmal sea
In which converge wild raving cosmic streams

That gutter in fantastic cataracts
To feed the swirling whirlpool-gulfs below.
As if supplied by black ensorcelled lamps,
A weird dark radiance illumines all;
And from the gulf, huge shadow-things arise—
Twin ebon-bodied winged leviathans
With twisted limbs and long colossal claws.
They gather up dark matter in the gloom,
And from that substance, raise a massive gate
By thaumaturgic gestures. From its arch
Weird vortices of ectoplasm pour,
And in the gyres, shapes of varied race
Rise up and multiply in manifold
Familiar shade—or take far stranger forms
Phantasmagoric, as in fever dream:
Of Titans, giants, gnomish folk, and imps,
And goblin beings, gargoyle-headed men;
And centaurs side-by-side with saurians,
Scale-tailed and crystal-eyed, in phantom ways;
And white arachnids, weirdly humanoid,
Which stride in spectral unison with things
Emerged from some mad god's menagerie—
Pale, luminescent algaes, many-eyed,
And faceless fungoid creatures, webbed and winged;
Odd floating orbs of psychic energy,
And other fabled forms innumerable,
Of otherworldly, unknown origins.
Now one thin wraith among the spectral throng—

Who is the only sample of his race—
Drifts forward as their sole ambassador,
And though he has no mouth with which to speak
I understand his language in my mind:

"We come in wonder, awe, and in our woe,
In death united and our knowledge pooled
(For what a shade has known all shades now know)
That one upon our portal is alive
Who treaded stars to seek our nebula:
Among our legions are the kings and queens,
The viziers, priests, and wizards, generals
Of dynasties long dead, which ruled in realms
On planets orbiting the million suns
Your almagests and testaments assign
As white Subhel, and golden Azimech,
Blue Algol, and pale rose Aldebaran;
As orange Fomalhaut and Betelgeuse,
And Cabalatrab, red and emerald green;
And Genib, Iclil, Menkar, Deneb, Thuban,
Zedaron, Zaurak, Zubenelgenubi:
The alphas, betas, gammas in your charts
Which form the signs and symbols of the night,
The iconography of zodiacs.
The merfolk who once lived in cities spread
Beneath eternal vaults of lunar ice;
The globe-like beings of gas giant worlds
Who dwelled and drifted in pacific zones

Dreams from a Black Nebula

Of atmosphere which like a cauldron brewed
Huge brooding storms that gathered gloom and churned
With centuries of crimson turbulence.
And others of an ever-changing shape
(For their true form is formlessness itself)
Who mimic those with whom they would converse;
And those who once inhabited no world
But flourished on the interstellar winds
Like motes of pollen borne upon the air;
And beings who once lived eternities
Perceived by others as a moment brief,
Like flashings of the subatomic sparks;
And others from an astral lineage
Who lived and died existences unseen
By those perceiving only matter's moulds;
And those enormous shadows over there,
Whose brows are furrowed by colossal glooms—
The ghostly pantheon of all our gods,
Whose avatars still haunt forgotten fanes
On worlds reclaimed by vast eternal night
In futile hope some acolyte of theirs
Might kindle at their altars some old faith.
Behold our ranks and files: the phantom host
That hails from sectors of the galaxy—
A spiral cluster, which, remotely viewed
From outer regions of the void, must seem
A mere amoeba in an ocean's mouth,

Whose own blind, futile gropings barely touch
The cold indifference of the universe."

The spirit legions all around me swirl
Like priests and ministers who would convene
An exorcism or some awful rite,
Discouraging my reeling mind with fear;
But speak instead the unimagined truths
Of lost religions, sciences and arts
Advanced by eon-ancient wizardries
They practiced once, and offer tutelage
In ways no sage or scholar could refuse . . .
But now their eldritch whisperings grow mute;
The vision fades, and rising from the fumes
That curl in primal chaos on my mind,
I hear a mausolean ocean's roar,
And in it, all the voices of the void
Break on emergent mist-enshrouded shores,
Disperse in hissing echoes, and recede
To voiceless shallows and the gloom-fed deeps.
All's silent now; again I am alone
Amid the vapors of a vanished dream.
The chamber walls and ceiling are restored;
My body has not moved, although I feel
A distance-ravaged traveler returned
To porch and portal in transfigured night.
And by the measure of an antique clock,
I know my voyage was a moment's dream
Evolved from out of only half a glass!

Dreams from a Black Nebula

I have the answer to my query now;
I must imbibe much deeper. I would know
The mysteries those hosts of ghosts would teach;
Upon the threshold of their ebon gate
I shall convoke and summon forth a guide
To lead the way beyond. Then will I be
Enlightened for a strange eternity,
Or overwhelmed by horror in the end?
I quaff the strange elixir once again
And shudder as a mist invades my mind.
Familiars! take from me these fleshy robes,
Then heap upon them these, my ancient bones—
This sorcerer departs!

Night Vigil for the Necromancer

I have here, master, leaves from your grimoire;
And by their elder glyphs and diagrams,
The arcane, overlapping pentagrams,
Surmise you voyage now the farthest shores
Where, singing spells of great antiquity,
You search for stranger necromantic lore
And chart the death dimension and its doors,
Those barriers between realities.

In your high castle carved from crystal verse,
A spectral servant waits for your return,
And speculates on what his lord might learn
In far, occult infinities immersed,
Where alien worlds emerge from nighted streams,
The unknown gulfs in nebulae of dream.

Green Wine of Xei Cambael

(After *Tales of the Dying Earth* by Jack Vance)

The placid sea is like a whispered psalm;
All rancor from the waves has sighed and ceased.
I sip green wine of Xei Cambael in peace.
My lips are numb; my limbs as if embalmed.
The dying sun is cool, but I am warm.
A third eye opens in my ancient brow;
The colors of the world seem clearer now
And paint a pastel realm removed from harm.

A pale green fairy murmurs to me songs
Of myths and fantasy my thoughts had lost—
Emergent now as from a permafrost
Like sad strange dreams dissolved in tints of mirth.
Together we muse not on right or wrong
While shadows spread across the dying earth.

Dragon

I've chased the dragon infinitely far
Through gulfs of time and realms of unknown space,
Beyond those limits most unwise to race—
Into the dragon's den, in distant stars
Where eon-watchers at the threshold deem
To keep his lair an occulted place,
To veil the shadow worlds from those who'd face
The wonders of his ancient dark regime.

But I have seen those heavens and red hells—
Those nebulae his avatars exhale
On emerald shores and vast obsidian lakes
Around that isle of blue jade citadels,
Where opalescent, curling vapors veil
The court in which the dreaming dragon wakes.

Barbarian

A smoke-laced sky is banner to our mirth
And sends our god red incense to inhale:
The sickly reek of sweat and blood-drenched earth
From savage tides of slaughter—spilled entrails,
Grim waves of flesh and feces, broken bone—
And clouds of flies, aswarm on butchered meat,
Are raising paean in demonic drone—
The voice of legion spawning in defeat.

Black vultures circle on their blade-like wings
As we collect our trophies from the dead
And stack colossal cairns of severed heads
Of which tonight our battlescribes will sing—
And valor, victory, triumphant death,
The charnel breeze that is our old god's breath.

Black Sabbath Sestina

Come, take my hand, child, I shall lead the way;
Of chosen few you are the chosen one.
In you, the fiery forges of true faith
Have built a black cathedral of your heart—
Wherein lie portals to the outer night
For which your heathen brethren here await.

The ancient altar in the woods awaits.
The stone is but a stage to open ways
For Those Who Dream beyond the wall of night.
Their many mysteries shall be as one
And known to you, within your soul and heart,
O most-unhallowed of uncommon faith.

All those who went before had lesser faith.
They are as shadows now; but they await,
In other spaces known to us by heart,
To guard and guide your spirit on its way;
But at the gate, there can be only one
To cross that threshold of transfigured night.

Your mind has fed upon essential night;
Your soul has drunk black oceans of our faith.
And as a child, you dreamed to be the one.
Assembled in the outer gulfs, They wait

And dream as you have for the open way.
The gate is locked; the key is in your heart.

You have no fear; in this we must take heart
As we prepare your journey into night.
The scriptures have described for us the way—
And you must find it, with a leap of faith,
Then reach that distant place where old gods wait
To greet the presence of a chosen one.

May all the nameless demons take this one,
This child who lives forever in our hearts!
We call upon the legions who await
To guide this creature through the voids of night,
On pale nocturnal voyage in pure faith,
And pray the sacrificed shall find her way,

For she shall lead us into utter night
By this, her bloody heart still pulsing faith,
Which like a black star, lights for Them the way!

Trans-Neptunian Shores

The sun is but a white star seen from here—
This barren orb of ice and rock terrain,
Where sovereign darkness and deep silence reign
In realm of thin mephitic atmosphere;
Where gelid, mauve-lit lakes of methane mist
Encircle cratered plains and crystal hills;
The jagged crags, like onyx citadels,
Whose keeps are gated by dark amethyst.

Beyond those gates are labyrinthine caves
That lead into a lower netherworld.
In that pitch blackness, nightmare things are curled
Like giant worms asleep in emptied graves—
Their dreams enfolded by eternal night,
Their black wings spread in transgalactic flight.

Lords of Chaos

Beyond black voids subsumed by blacker fire
We conjure entities from gates of hell;
And knowing all their names impose our will,
Binding those spirits with essential night
To glean the mysteries of eldritch dark
Which warp the weave of time and space and earth.

Our dreams are of dominion over earth:
With minds immersed in metaphysic fires
Which emanate from realms in outer dark,
We shape hallucinations out of hell
And mould the minds of men with fear of night,
Making them kneel before our very will.

With black theurgic arts and iron will,
We raise lost dynasties of elder earth
And call dead gods from nebulae of night.
With eyes agleaming necromantic fire,
Our ancestors and deities of hell,
Shall rise like shadows from supernal dark.

All things shall shift towards eternal dark,
Disordered by entropic force of will.
Our priests and prophets, praising highest hell,
Shall spread unholy gospel over earth

Where lords of darkness wield phantasmal fires
Beneath a vault of vast sepulchral night.

The days will be returned to endless night;
The sun and all the stars shall glut the dark
With all their finite, final astral fires
Accelerated by our burning will,
And shadow will occult a dying earth
Where mortals bow before the lords of hell.

Humanity, impelled by laws of hell,
Shall submit beneath the rune and seal of night;
Chaos will flower over sea and earth,
And wraith-like winds shall sweep throughout the dark,
Directed by the fancies of our will
From where we laugh upon our thrones of fire.

Our will and ideas burn with spectral fire
In visions of a dark and rising hell
Where infinite night has swept away the earth.

Hwamgaarl,
the City of Screaming Statues

(After *The Elric Saga* by Michael Moorcock)

Built from huge blocks of green obsidian,
Old Hwamgaarl's hundred twisted towers rise
Like talons scraping at black magic skies.
Few foreigners have visited within;
Most flee before the city walls, where stand
Weird testaments to sorcery in stone:
The screaming statues—tortured souls which moan
Strange litanies in voices of the damned.

Throughout the city statues shout and scream,
Submerging streets in sobbing waves of pain;
And here inhabitants are all insane,
Who hearing, heed disturbed religious dreams
And serve black shrines where chaos gods are praised
And pale demonian entities are raised.

Dead Meadow

There lies a field beyond the potter's field,
A meadow blanketed by soft black mold;
Where blood-red lichens take a creeping hold
On soil once fertile, bountiful in yield.
Here pallid, baleful flowers of disease
Push up from nightmare origins unknown
To breathe a sickly odor on the breeze
And send dark spores across the poisoned zone.

Old rustics knowing well the region tell
Of warlocks who were burned and buried there.
They say the meadow is a door to hell
From which vile spirits rise and walk the air
Like shadows out of vengeful evil dreams,
To weird the withered field and taint the streams.

IN SPECTRAL
PROVINCES

Plutonian

With night's eternal blackness for a dome,
The surface here seems subterranean—
A tholin-dusted, shadowed crystal plain
That dimly glitters in a star-lit gloam
Where giant adamantine gates seclude
Dark ice-hewn courtyards from the phantom sun,
Which mocks the realm at cold aphelion
Forever sealed in cryptic solitude.

Occulted on the rim, it is a tomb—
A world of wraiths ruled by a sovereign ghost.
And astral on the Acherontic stream,
I voyage to its unknown shores of gloom,
For I would hear the oracles that host
Would speak to me in necromantic dreams.

Event Horizon

How perfect and symmetrical the sphere
Our ageless, vast galactic center holds:
That god-like, ebon countenance so cold,
Devouring all substance it draws near.
From that black maw where orbs are thrown accursed,
Astronomers on other, outer worlds
Detect dim voices that once voidward hurled,
Translated into cosmic X-ray bursts.

Long since we crossed the Schwarzschild radius;
Our planet drifts a black abyssal sea
As prophets howl the darkness cleanses us
Before the altar of dark deity—
That our lost tribes are now returning home
To undimensioned realms where phantoms roam.

Solarized

The sun again was god, so we returned
To ancient ways and bowed in solar prayer,
Abandoning all earthly hope and cares
Before the benediction rite—then burned.
Now bathed in ebon light of black hole suns,
No longer limited by laws of mass,
We witness other orbs eternally pass
Into their various oblivions.

Pale sentinels, we wander through the voids
And violet gulfs of spectral nebulae,
Where darker, greener valleys are arrayed
With young gods, whose orbiting planetoids
Hold new alien races in their time
Of worship to false ghosts beyond the primes.

Return at Evening

Dream not that I shall not return
As if to walk in worlds apart;
But stir my ashes in their urn—
My ghost from you shall not depart.

If I must walk in worlds apart,
Just leave for me a little light:
My ghost from you shall not depart,
I'll only leave the day for night.

Just leave for me a little light.
My apparition shall appear.
I'll only leave the day for night,
In twilight as the evening nears.

My apparition shall appear,
Just stir the ashes in my urn.
In twilight as the evening nears,
Dream not that I shall not return.

Nocturne

Do you hear, child of the moon,
Drifting under Saturn's sign,
That melancholy tune
From where Pleiadean stars align?

The weirdly haunting, alien tones
Drift moth-like from some neverwhere,
Fluttering through the ether zones,
The haunted hyacinthine air.

Out of body and somber mood,
Your fugue-like spirit floats,
Lifted from its solitude
On star-winds and phantasmal motes!

Listen, child of the moon, let us see
What crawls from Night's menagerie.

Ghost Sonata

Remember my ghost, standing there
Before the moondawn's noon eclipse,
The kisses you drank with your sky blue lips
From the windwraith weaving the web of air?

We wandered in the labyrinth
In deep green shadows of the noon,
When the nimbus spread across the moon
Like a liquid pearl of green absinthe.

Remember, beneath our naked feet
The forest's floor of murmurous moss,
The pale blue mushrooms and emerald gloss
That glowered glad with an alien heat?

And remember, the mist and rain
That mingled with the moonbeam rays?
The silvered violets, the pale green grays . . .
Or does it seem now but a purple stain?

Remember, child of the moon? Do
You see, from where the vines enclose,
The scene unfolds as a steel blue rose,
Gathering dreams from the cobweb's dew?

Eclogue

Did I see you, ghost, in the glade,
When we trod the dull red amber foam,
Where the soft, deep, strawberry shade
Enfolds the yellow glowworm's gloam?

An iron orchid's remnant dream
Laid molten on the jade glass lawn.
I remember the sibilant stream;
And still, the star-like flowers spawn.

On the lilac's lashes fluttered ghosts
Of palest blue ephemerals;
And the roses curled like scarlet hosts
In the crysalid dream of emeralds.

I see you, ghost; the moonbeams blur
You. I heard your phantom *Te Deums* . . .
Or was it the willow's murmur,
Above the chrome chrysanthemums?

Nature Unveiled

—After Poe

Now we roam the other regions
Where the long black shadows fall
Beneath a dim nocturnal sun,
Far beyond the outer wall.

Where the long black shadows fall,
The dreams of men exist no more;
Far beyond the outer wall
Our legions cross the farthest shore.

The dreams of men exist no more;
All the unknown is now known.
Our weary legions cross the shore
To strange flat fields that we have sown.

All the unknown is now known
In silence of a dreamless vale
And strange flat fields that we have sown
Beyond the shade of nature's veil.

Silent is the dreamless vale
Beneath a dim nocturnal sun
Beyond the shade of nature's veil
Where we roam the other regions.

Dreams from a Black Nebula

Dreams in the Lich House

In outer dark of dreams I'm summoned there,
Across the valleys veiled in charnel gloom—
A giant house within a world of tombs,
Wherein the lich-queens sit on rune-carved chairs
In death-like state, with eerie elegance—
Each wearing rotted, regal yellow gowns,
Their tomb-sprung hair beneath black iron crowns,
Their green eyes gleaming live malevolence.

In death that is not death the liches dream
To rule new realms, and reach beyond their own
By sorcery in search of other thrones . . .
In dreaming me, the undead witches deem
To whisper lore of legacies that loom
In hidden vaults of black and eldritch dooms.

The Barrow in the Highlands

When travelers pass through this haunted land,
The barrow seems another grassy mound
Except for mossy, shattered stones around—
A circle which no longer upright stands.
Upon the stones inscriptions can be found
In some old tongue inscribed by unknown hands.
Few passersby—save locals—understand
They tread a track that lies near hallowed ground.

And few are those who gather here on nights
When all is weirdly lit by full moon phase
To mark a cleric's laying of a curse
On one interred here in the olden days,
Who rules his ancient worshippers a wight
Before dawn's glimmerings their shades disperse.

Dreams from a Black Nebula

Ghost Mountains

(Gamburtsev Mountain Range, 80° 30´ S., 76° 00´ E.)

Above white wastes, the spectral southern lights
Illume no reaches of a hidden range,
Where mountains rise mysterious and strange
Beneath dark miles of old Antarctic ice.
On maps which chart those bleak sub-glacial deeps
Are valleys of enigma, lakes and rifts—
Where psychics warn primeval terror sleeps,
Awaiting cataclysmic climate shifts:

In dreams they see the continent in thaw,
Releasing from the frozen vaults of time
Unearthly life forms, pooling like black slime . . .
In visions, they perceive with cosmic awe
Great mausolean pinnacles arise,
And graveless things which flood auroral skies.

Succubus

I'll slip into your sleeping soul
As a pale, mysterious dream
In which all unknown pleasures seem
Within your power to control;

You'll sip the philtre of my kiss,
And unholy joy will flood your heart
As I apply demonic art,
Quenching your appetite's abyss.

But I extract a price, my dear:
After your energy is spent,
And I have drained your love like wine,
I'll crush your fantasy—in fear,

You'll recognize from where I'm sent,
But by then, your soul is damned—and mine.

Night Winds

As twilight falls, the night winds rise
From other regions white as bone.
Like spirits from auroral skies,
They roam the tundra's treeless zones
With eerie moans and evil shrieks;
All night, the weird white waste they seek

In chorus, chanting some strange call
Like music of the outer spheres—
A vague, demonian music all
At first confused, then crystal clear:
The otherworld now summons me
To roam the wastelands, dead and free.

"Curst be he yt moves my bones"

A curse upon the one that moves my bones,
On him who dares my slumber desecrate
Despiting imprecation in gray slate,
Who heeds not words engraved upon this stone.
Chthonic gods and daemons, oversee
This pious dweller of the twilight void,
And see disturbers of his tomb destroyed,
Then buried not with rites of piety.

And if the deities heed not my prayer,
I weird my corpse a revenant, with mould
For brains and tomb-dust clotted hair,
And force these lifeless limbs with strength to hold
My haunted foe unto unhallowed grave,
To clear the path of vengeance I shall pave.

Dreams from a Black Nebula

De Vermis Mysteriis

How black the soil, of this your hallowed ground,
Wherein unknown for eons you have lain;
The realm in which my rotted soul was found
And resurrected in your corpse-fed fane.
I am your true priest, symbiotic host
Who worships you as you were meant to be;
Who hooks the lowly hordes upon your ghost
With promise of a mindless ecstasy:

Upon the earth dark ecstasy shall flood,
Fulfilling your black will and nightmare need.
As parasites that rage in living blood,
The poor and famished in your faith shall feed,
Transform the world in undulating waves
Like writhing worms that grope within the grave.

Inscriptions

Embalmed, in cerements, I sleep;
Once I walked as a living god.
My sepulcher from sight still keeps
My amulets and ruling rod;
And on my casket nenuphars
Of pearl and opal gleam like stars.

These deeds inscribed upon the lid
Are interspersed with charms and spells,
The secrets of the pyramids
And holy scripture, which foretells
Of other worlds awaiting us
Beyond the black sarcophagus.

How strange are the eons still unslept
In voyage to the Western Lands;
How strange were the tears of those who wept
To follow me across the sands,
Across the Night's great unknown sea,
In search of greater mystery.

Dreams from a Black Nebula

Necuratul

Forsaken for these centuries
Not dead, but dreaming, have I lain;
And mine is metaphysic pain,
God's curse upon my ministry
And name that bears Satanic stains.

With limbs as thin as withered reeds
And talons long as coffin nails,
I rise from sleep beyond the pale,
Leaving my grave beneath the weeds
To seek the simple, sick and frail;

And under dim nocturnal suns,
I summon minions from the breeds
Of scuttling vermin, as they feed
On lesser life and carrion,
And preach my pestilential creed.

And ever as I stalk beneath
The black skies vaulted like a tomb,
I gaze on God's eternal gloom
And mutter through my needle teeth
The mantra of my cult of doom:

A truth, transmitted by the fleas,
Which turns the dying from His light—
The bitten are my cenobites,
Who spread my gospel like disease
And teach the word of death and night.

SONGS FROM THE NAMELESS HERMITAGE

We have seen the black suns
Pouring forth the night.

—Clark Ashton Smith

The Eremite

On moonless nights when stars are crystal clear
And shadows settle gently in the calm
Around my unlit hut, I raise weird psalms
In praise of blacker gulfs beyond the spheres;
And when the world is at its quietest,
I walk with voiceless entities unseen
Who hear my hymns from where they roam between
The known dimensions and the alien rest.

A hermit of remotest wastes, I stand
In reverence to what the darkness brings—
My songs are spells negating falser light
Illumining all temples in the land,
And prophets know the sable songs I sing
Are songs of black suns pouring forth the night.

A Vessel for Black Waters

Out in the wasteland in the days before
The solstices, I journey to the caves
Which hold monastic bones in hidden graves
Beneath the table of a windswept moor.
The ceremonies that I here perform
Were well-known once, but long-forgotten now—
Except by few who share a sacred vow
To see this world by prophecy reformed.

Attuned to distant voices here entombed,
I am an empty vessel, mute and still,
Through which the spirits speak and guide my quill—
This way an elder wisdom is exhumed
From scriptures long-since lost in holy wars,
And wise men call the books I write grimoires.

Brotherhood of the Black Waters

When seven faceless monks all robed in black
Paid visit to the village and held mass,
They spoke of elder brethren who had passed
Beyond into the void—and one returned.
In rituals all infants were divined;
Then they announced that they had found their haunt—
So baptized me within the eldritch font
Of ebon waters channeled from their minds.

They taught true knowledge was remembering
And trained my memory in sacred lore—
Then raised the currents of my lives before,
Which flowed like night from otherworldly springs
And rippled with the telepathic flames
Of voices blessing me with many names.

Tombs of the Dead Gods

In some black hollow of the multiverse
Exists the graveyard where the dead gods dream:
The primal pantheon that ruled supreme
Before their hierarchies were reversed—
Their temples razed and clergies overthrown
And sacrificed in untold hecatombs,
As minor idols, now like giants, loomed
And new gods sat upon their borrowed thrones.

Survivors of the holocaust kept faith,
Believing that in death their gods but sleep
In Time's great ocean, dwelling eons deep—
And nought are eons to eternal wraiths.
Vast revolutions of the Cosmic Wheel
Shall see their starry crypts in space unsealed.

Procession

From world to world old wisdom made its way—
The esoteric rites and runes preserved
By one black order from the undeserved
Beneath each new sun's false corrupting rays.
But epochs saw the knowledge was dispersed;
The canon fragmented; now incomplete,
Our brethren keep the shards with faith replete,
In waters of obsidian immersed:

Beyond all space and time, an ocean still;
And as it is above it is below.
By subtle currents and strange undertow,
Its vassals are as vessels to be filled,
And to the voice of many waters turn—
We serve the dead gods till their ghosts return.

Dreams from the Black Nebula

Engraved in shards of emerald are runes
That name the dead gods—black suns pouring all
The echoes of a greater ocean's call
To which the souls of acolytes attune;
And these are blessed to hear the cosmic lull—
Those waters of annihilating grace
Beyond a cloud obscuring that annuls
All light that reaches regions of that space.

And dreams emerge from that black nebula—
Transmissions for the mind of smooth blank slate,
In symbols, signs and seals that I translate,
Configure with hermetic formulas
To raise my soul into the boundless lake,
Where rivers of my dreams merge in Their wake.

Night Songs

Through lesser channels of dark theurgy,
The legions of the outer night attend;
The lunar spectra warp and shadows bend
To songs invoking evening synergy—
And apparitions to my region throng
From mansions on remotest astral planes
In eldritch chorus, calling in refrain
With void-like harmonies of voiceless song.

And in that very voicelessness is heard
The eons echoed in abyssal wells—
Like waveless waves of lulling song that spell
Negating syllables of primal word.
I hear the soundless song and thus I know
The wellspring from which cosmic darkness flows.

In Term

My elders sought their unknown origins
Through clouds dissolving earthly matters known.
A star absorbing night where it was sown,
I walk the ebon road that leads within,
And rise unto occulted outer gates
Where all things shall return in cyclic course—
A primal realm of unbegotten source,
The formless field that forms and discreates.

It is pure presence: vast and black and void
Of otherness, of intellect destroyed.
Beyond the temples where the false converge,
I leave the falser icons far behind
And reach black sanctums, where I seek to find
Perfection in the mindless demiurge.

Astronomy Domine

Removed from ways of men, no city lights
Encroach upon my shadowed quietude.
In soft black silence, veiled in solitude,
I train my telescopes into the night
Where seedling suns in nebulae are sown;
And by the old and new astrologies,
I calculate the untold destinies
There written in the black sea's astral zones.

Tonight the nearest planets are aligned;
They gleam like hellish rubies, and the stars
So weirdly in the welkin shine like eyes
As I behold a strange emblazoned sign—
A comet vectored like a scimitar
In constellations where the gods shall rise.

Black Suns

I kneel as many who have knelt before
The dead gods wandering through gulfs afar
In distant isolation—sundered stars
As chronicled in astronomic lore.
My soul extends to those extinguished shores,
As drawn by tidal calls of magnetars—
Each oceanic voice, an avatar
Embodied in its remnant carbon core.

These nighted suns are cold perfected spheres—
Dark planetary diamonds without flaw,
Reflecting black abysses smooth as glass
From which phantasmagoria is cleared
By ban of absolute eternal law
Beneath which Being and all Time shall pass.

Apparitions of Astral Night

Illusions spawn beneath the dying sun—
Bright lies that lead the lay as creatures blind
From truth in darkness risen out of mind,
The emanations of the outer One.
How false the light upon the desert's sea—
The strange oases of mirage, that send
White priests to search for evanescent ends,
To taste the dust of unreality.

The apparitions of the astral night
Would lead those desert walkers to the shade
Of black irradiation from beyond.
Beyond the light, they guide the anchorite
Towards the source from which his soul is made,
To ripple in the still and darkling pond.

Revelation in Black

In dreams I saw autumnal equinox—
The red sun and the blue sun stood opposed
As minor orbs and major moons arose
In equal day and night. The skies unlocked
The oceans of the interstellar wastes
That flooded forth in black eclipsing seas;
As I recalled old verse and sanctities,
Lost prophets rose from sepulchers displaced.

Upon their brows were blazing solar seals;
Sublunar shadows multiplied as spawn
Of Night essential, calling forth her brood
By sorcery to see her rune revealed:
A black sun on the weird horizon stood;
Supernal darkness on the world had dawned.

ANOMALIES

The Kin Fetch

Last of his line, he returned
to his ancestral home,
haunted by inheritance.

She had been there so long
that she wore the house like clothes.
Sometimes there was a stench,
and he thought he saw her,
like a gray thought
moving through the many rooms
and closets of his mind.

She never slept inside
(that was done in the family crypt)
but would visit in the night,
watching him breathe
as the moon rose in the sky,
patient as a glacier
laying its long cold arms on the land
inevitably all its own.

Supernatural Refugees

We are the unseemly ghosts.

We are the shadows
who are unable to become fully spectral,
the summoned spirits
who produce no ectoplasm.
We are poltergeists who
have no energy to stack furniture
in bizarrely balanced columns
or raise whirlwinds in livingrooms.

We are the not-so-possessive spirits who
make exorcists laugh in relief;
the unhungry ghosts
who fail to appear at seance tables.
We are the ones
who let down the spiritualists,
fail to convert sceptics,
and cause the paranormal researcher
to lay down her instruments
and sigh.

We are the supernaturally dispossessed:
persecuted as heretics and freaks,
we've been hounded from the otherworld,

and our immaterial multitudes

are shuffling to the border of your realm,

harmless as shadow puppets

and too weary

to rattle our chains at the gate.

We only seek asylum in your abandoned houses

and forgotten attics,

in the closets of your dreams.

The Propagule

The old man steps off the passenger bus
and heads towards the forest's edge.
No one on board notices
the gray shadow on the empty seat.
It's twilight as the old man
moves between the trees, boots treading
on the silent soft brown earth.
Mushrooms sprout in his footsteps.
Black jelly fungi and colorful slime molds
begin to spread over tree and stone.
Large brain-like bodies swell in the gloom
while gray and ochre mildews multiply
in nurturing mist.
The man looks around him, then moves on;
the fruiting fungoids follow him.
Soon streams clot, roots rot;
the forest deadens, decomposes,
turns to swamp. As night blooms around him,
the old man bursts into a cloud of spores
even as mist and moon mold over,
and the evening sky glows oddly phosphorescent,
emerald green.

Thing of Spring

(After "Witches in Winter" by Darrell Schweitzer)

Those aren't flowers,
the oddly mottled buds peeking
just above the soil,
in the garden back rows,
as dawn slowly burns away the shadows
and the other plants
writhe in a curious susurrus.

Those aren't flowers,
flowering, unfolding dewy petals
as the birds shriek terribly
at wormish squirmings in the earth,
as the insects trill
shrill, cacophonous litanies
while the gardener stirs from sleep,
a nightmare seed still rooted in dream,
developing weird shoots,
efflorescent tendrils creeping everywhere.

Those aren't flowers.

Mooncalf

Not so much birthed as
aborted by something
absolute, it arrived
among them much unloved

by the shambling herd.
It suckled no milk,
thirsted some great otherness.
Nudged, it stumbled out

of the tremulous barn
wobbly-kneed, wandered
beyond the pale hedgerows
into open pasture

untroubled by thoughts
and chewed on shadows,
drank from a swirling shallow
cribbed in space.

It was found in a field
like a cloud-blotted moon,
withholding origins.
The older ones would read

Dreams from a Black Nebula

omens of some other world
in a wormholed morn,
the odd-numbered nubs
on a flawed, unhallowed head.

Dunwich Pastoral

Your inherited thoughts,
like deformed birds
twittering in a fog
that clouds your brain.

You ignore the shadow of
demented offspring
at the upper window,
the toad-throated voice

and gibberish song
that drove you outside,
nerves now whittled down
to inbred bones.

The stones of the well
are cool to the touch;
the soft black water soothes,
unclots your head.

As the mist begins to lift
from the blasted heath,
you settle like a leaf
on needful deeds,

hearing the swaying pines
in still night air,
the rumblings from the hill,
the ground below.

The Worm Conjurer

The old one drives a stob
into damp brown sod
then rubs the teeth of a saw
on the end of the post

to work weird music
from the sapling wood:
the movements of a maestro
on the oddest violin.

Thus the lowly ones are called,
leaving their burrows
in earth's dark abdomen.
Soon the forest's floor

is swarming with them,
the fiddler at the center
of a crawling radius.
He kneels to gather the wealth.

We come to him
when our thin white bait won't lure,
with belief and oaths
of magic on our tongues.

Anadromous

We waited for the bloody sun to scab
before breaching the murky surface,
flopping ourselves onto the pink-frothed banks
of our chem-polluted natal stream.

Janet croaked, and pointed out a place.
I kept close by, watchful of predators
as she squatted to deposit her eggs—
a fist-sized basket of rubies in the mud.

I leaned over them and vomited my milt.
Then we covered our secret treasure trove.
There was nothing more for us do.
We turned bright red and floated dead downstream.

Weavers

We woke to find whole towns in gossamer.
The forests ghostly, veiled in gauze. The bodies
of men and beasts inhumed like mummies
in weird weavework seemingly woven of moonlight.

From the hills, town and country looked snow-shrouded.
At distance we watched Them moving in mist—
eldritch spinners coming and going,
restless architects of the demonweb.

Then in winter the awful arachnids died;
it seemed the horror had run its course.
We set to clearing the nightmare threads away.
But soon the cocooned bodies stirred. Then hatched.

Old Growth

When we have stood too long
in the heart of the woods,
and finally wake
from our long, slow dreams
in the green shadow that is our soul;

When we discover the horror
of the multitudes felled in slumber;

When we who are many and one
remember our roots
and return to ways of movement,
the sound of swaying timber
and the whispers of a million lips of green
will carry on twilight winds
like the roar of the sea.

You will not notice
how the forest's edge
moves closer in the night.

Golem Variant

The ancient rabbi's voice
like a ghost
stirring amid the ashes of long-
dead speech.

A lump of matter in a circle.

The chamber trembles
with waves of
incantatory activity.
The servant, turning grave,
raises a hand
to shield his eyes against the light
as ritual
augments tissue . . .

mutations later:

"I'll fetch the shovel, sir."

An unformed mouth swallowing the night.

From Tindalos

It's not a dream.

You've been sleepwalking through
ancestral forests,
transplanted so long ago
on this terraformed moon.
And it would be Beltane
back on Earth, had it
not lost the strange temptation
to exist.

As the distant sun, blood-red
and nearly dead,
sinks behind Saturn's rim,
twilight comes with baleful howls of
hounds that hail not
from Anwynn's fairy realm,
but beyond time's angle
and the silent curvature of space.

And you know you can only wait
at this pre-established spot
among the trees,
where star-winds blow

ashes of extinguished worlds
through the dark, nebulous boughs
of your branching memory—
the source of psychic scent they seek
from Tindalos.

Dreams from a Black Nebula

Brood of the Black Goat

Beyond the wood,
the newborn black goats.

In their yellow eyes,
the vacuity of innocence.
In the hollows
of their hoofprints,
abyssal pools.

To the sound of
a thousand lost voices
crying in the night,
something vast, old,
and shapeless
moves behind the stars.

Between the spring
and the fountain:
the membrane of space,
tissue-thin
but eons deep.

To the bleating,
a nameless shepherd comes
to tend the flock.

Overheard at a Wharfside Tavern

They hopped and flopped and croaked
but weren't toads. Sure,
toads come green, but got no gills.
No scales or flippers, neither;
and some were big as dogs. Worst of all:
their starfish heads. When we docked the boat,
beach was full of them. Jenkins
didn't seem surprised,
just set to drying out the nets.
"Seen it before, back in '69," he says.
"They come up from coral caverns in the deep."
"But what're they doin'?" says I.
He just shrugs. "Breedin', likely."
With one eye on the beach, I got to work.
Snagged myself on a red hook
and had queer thoughts about the mingled blood.
When the fish were clean and packed on ice,
I dumped the gut buckets overboard.
That drew 'em out. Gulls never had a chance.
Them things swam out fast and swarmed,
churning up crimson whirlpools. Then they were gone.
Couldn't sleep that night.
In the blue horror of daybreak
I drifted into dream,
out beyond the blackness of the reef.

The Necklace

Without a doubt, he likes his drink;
But then, consider his grim trade:
By lantern-light to wield a spade—
Imagine how the office stinks!

But I believe the story true
About that night he came to meet
The richest dame he ever knew,
The one who set him up so nice and neat.

He told me at the Grinning Goat
(We always did our business there)
How her fresh corpse had grabbed his throat;

To verify, he showed me where
He feels a spectral hand still clutch—
The marks are black, and cold to touch.

Gothic Blue Book

A castle, built on ruins—the first scene:
In secret tunnels burrowed through the earth
Or lost foundations—for symbolic worth;
Perhaps an apparition here is seen.
A tempest in a tenebrous sky is good;
The wailing wind, as psychic metaphor,
Might lash our heroine who, splashed with gore,
Is running wildly in subconscious woods.

Insert extremes of human passion here—
Maybe forsaken vows, forbidden lust;
Perhaps a tomb-tryst in the charnel dust.
Maintain that strange, penumbral atmosphere.
Add omens, or an old ancestral curse;
Some premonitions of a trundling hearse.

Dreams from a Black Nebula

The Stains

The stains began to grow upon the walls;
we barely noticed when they first appeared.
Just patches of innocuous gray smears—
or so we thought, before they claimed the halls,
corrupted everything at quickened pace:
dark smudges spread; black lichens crept and veined
the ceiling, floors and rooms, so when it rained
a fetid odor swamped our living place.
In withered days, we started growing thin
as all the food had moldered to the last.
Resignedly, in languor of the fast,
we watched the evil stains take to our skin.
The roof fell in and will not be repaired.
We need for nothing now but cool night air.

Classical Revenant

Verily, she returned that night
hours after he left her grave—
a cool, malicious memory
following him like moon-drawn waves.

That night he felt a phantom touch
whilst tippling to his recent cheer;
upon the mantle in the den
her lovely portrait seemed to sneer.

That night, forsooth, he was assailed
by many ghostly horror tropes;
surely, strange planets were passing through
the houses of his horoscope!

That night his dreams were led astray
to moonpools on an astral path . . .
he met a beckoning fair one there. . . .
They found him bloated in the bath.

Remembrancer of the Bibliognostic Hippocamp

(For Derrick Hussey)

O Keeper of forbidden scrolls of doom,
Librarian of weird and arcane lore,
who knows the cryptic runes of rare grimoires
and wards deep mystery in vaults of gloom,
you hold the hieroglyphic prophecies
from one old wizard of the eldritch dark
who wrote of Beauty and the demon's mark—
I seek his vintage verse in volumes three.

Great visions raised from infinite black wells,
communications with an elder race
long dead but dreaming out of Time and Space—
such wisdom in that tripled tome of spells
make all the other books on my shelves seem
the impotent work of minds that never dreamed!

The Sales Pitch

It's true the place is like a crumbling tomb
and the garden's gone to hell, but inside
I'm sure you'll find it all as specified:
there's something wrong with almost every room.
The fixtures come with it. The paintings scream
unnervingly at night, as if in pain;
the parlor's well-imbued with psychic stains.
Here's the bedroom. You said you'd like bad dreams;
those heavy footsteps on the upper floor
are likely from the thirteen suicides—
in sleep you're sure to see the blood-red tides
that flood the halls and pour out through the doors.
The cellar harbors dark abyssal fear.
I'm glad you like the place. Now just sign here.

Chimera Park

Sometimes I take a stroll down to the park
to view the ever-changing foliage
where alien botanists have turned the page
on what we knew of nature's matriarch.
Guards lock the gate before it gets too dark,
when all the mutant flora start to rage
like surrealists at the bars of reason's cage,
releasing fauna from some unknown ark.

All night the gibbering things spar and spawn
like irrational shapes in dreams that range
in pasture far beyond our sanity;
but in the first dispelling rays of dawn
their curious groping forms begin to change
back to weird plants, fantastic flowers and trees.

The Priest of P'rea

(For Danny Lovecraft)

In some remote, well-hidden cavern lit
By wizard sorcery and candlelight,
Demonic shapes take form and shadow-flit
On spectral wings into the austral night.
Here a high priest of P'rea meditates
On arcane symbols, metaphors of fear.
In this retreat he prays, and contemplates
The dark illuminations of the Weird.

About him lie Alexandrian scrolls
And well-thumbed grimoires bound in dragon hide,
From which tonight arise a voice-like tide—
As if a vast, oracular ocean rolls
The poetry of lost worlds to his dunes
Transmitted by dim ghosts on distant moons.

Nightfall in Sesqua

(for W. H. Pugmire)

Deep in the woodland, now that day departs,
A subtle sentience in dreamlife stirs
Among the hemlocks, pines and Douglas firs
As cryptic gloom enfolds the valley's heart.
Dim starlight falls; but only silence speaks
As mist encircles all the elder growth,
The trees like cenobites in sacred oath
Before Mt. Selta's wing-like, white twin peaks.

Dark creatures rise now from a darker sleep—
They dance around an obelisk of stone,
Piping weird songs on flutes of human bone
In praise of One Who Dreams in cosmic deeps;
And summoned to their throng by mournful howls
Flit the white shadows of observant owls.

Inquisition on the Dunes

Tattooed with hieroglyphic spells, she waits
Beneath the ghostly necromantic moons,
Which flood the vast, forsaken desert dunes,
Where solemnly she sits to meditate.
On astral voyage, she arrives at gates
And mutters at their locks a mantic rune,
Then sends her songs of summons through—and soon
An alien genie leaves its far estate.

And as that giant phantom of the flames
Arises as a pillar of black fumes,
The sorceress from purpose never veers—
Demanding all the numbers and the names
Of demons dreaming in occulted tombs
Who influence the movements of the spheres.

Atlach-Nacha

No humanoids his machinations sense—
He moves between dimensions and dark space
With silent, alien, arachnid grace
In strange eternal search for sustenance.
The mind behind his battery of eyes
Would fill the void of one vast abdomen—
A well where souls of women, children, men
Abate old hunger that can never die.

Like beads of dew upon a silky thread,
Our worlds are caught within a cosmic dream—
Where to this elder god, the planets seem
Mere multi-colored cocoons—a banquet spread
Before its evil, cold insectile sight,
Beneath his shadow of essential night.

Monastic Ruins

The chapel stood in twilight mist obscured
As solemn as a specter in its shroud;
The ruined edifice still grim and proud,
Its iron door now open at my word.
No watcher stood in wait to warn or halt
A weary entity, accursed and foul,
Who now returned and by dark shadows cowled
Descended to the vast sepulchral vault.

There, in the silent language of the dead,
I sought before my elders to atone;
And murmurs rose up from their mouldered bones
To utter ancient edicts that had said
All worlds forever would I roam, in quest
For absolution and eternal rest.

Divine Invasion

The signs emerged the night before:
Throughout the northern hemisphere
Astronomers went raving mad.
The governments urged calm, not fear

Despite the evil effluence
That ebbed out from the planetoid
So new to our blue atmosphere,
That all our nukes could not destroy.

Days passed; the rock receded back
Into the gulf from which it came.
Through pale green fog that wreathed the world
Then strode the gods without a name.

90482 Orcus

Beyond the circle Neptune holds
And centaur's cometary reach,
No clamor mars the ebon beach
Where Orcus reigns in darkness old.

Here netherworldly sentinels
Patrol the monarch's muted shores
As nightfall everlasting pours
From outer rims of cosmic hells;

And Vanth, on tholin-dusted wings,
Remote in vigil outermost,
Forever leads unworlded ghosts
Through voids to greet their gloomy king.

Acknowledgments

"Anadromous," *Star*Line* 34.1 (2010).

"Astral Hierarchy," *Nameless* No. 2 (2012).

"Barbarian," *Heroic Fantasy Quarterly* No. 16 (2013).

"Beyond the Wall of Tsang," *Dreams and Nightmares* No. 95 (2013).

"The Black Abbess," *Weird Fiction Review* No. 3 (2012).

"The Black Idol," *Weird Fiction Review* No. 2 (2011).

"Black Sabbath Sestina," *Star*Line* 36.2 (2013).

"Brood of the Black Goat," *Dreams and Nightmares* No. 83 (2009).

"Château Nevreant," *Space and Time* No. 121 (2014).

"Chimera Park," *Star*Line* 34.4 (2011).

"December in the Druid Woods," *Nameless* No. 2 (2012).

"The Demon Sea," *Weird Fiction Review* No. 3 (2012).

"De Vermis Mysteriis," *Weird Fiction Review* No. 5 (2014).

"Divine Invasion," *Abyss and Apex* (September 2012).

"Dunwich Pastoral," *Dreams and Nightmares* No. 87 (2010).

"Eclogue," *Black Petals* No. 45 (2008).

"The Eremite," *Nameless* No. 2 (2012).

"Event Horizon," *Abyss and Apex* (March 2012).

"From Tindalos," *Space and Time* No. 109 (2009).

"Ghost Sonata," *Black Petals* No. 45 (2008).

"Golem Variant," *Dreams and Nightmares* No. 83 (2009).

"Gothic Blue Book," *Star*Line* 36.4 (2013).

"Green Wine of Xei Cambael," *Star*Line* 36.1 (2013).

"The Kin Fetch," *Dreams and Nightmares* No. 90 (2011).

"Lords of Chaos," *A Darke Phantastique*, ed. Jason V Brock (Cycatrix Press, 2014).

"Monastic Ruins," *Tales from the River* No. 1 (2012).

"Mooncalf," *Star*Line* 33.4 (2010).

"Moonflowers," *Nameless* No. 1 (2012).

"The Necklace," *Dreams and Nightmares* No. 95 (2013).

"The Necromantic Wine," *Avatars of Wizardry*, ed. Charles Love-craft (P'rea Press, 2012).

"Necuratul," *Star*Line* 36.4 (2013).

"New Lost Worlds," *Weird Fiction Review* No. 2 (2011).

"Nocturne," *Black Petals* No. 45 (2008).

"Old Growth," *Space and Time* No. 112 (2010).

"90482 Orcus," *Star*Line* 35.2 (2012).

"Overheard at a Wharfside Tavern," *Dreams and Nightmares* No. 85 (2010).

"Plutonian," *Nameless* No. 1 (2012).

"The Propagule," *Hidden (Not One of Us)* (2010).

"Prophecy of the Red Death," *Weird Fiction Review* No. 5 (2014).

"Return at Evening," *Dreams and Nightmares* No. 89 (2011).

"The Sales Pitch," *ParABnormal Digest* No. 2 (2011).

"Shadow and Silence," *Nameless* No. 1 (2012).

"Solarized," *Abyss and Apex* (June 2012).

"Spectral Province." *Spectral Realms* No. 1 (2014).

"The Stains," *ParABnormal Digest* No. 1 (2011).

"Starry Wisdom," *Star*Line* 35.1 (2012).

"Succubus," *Strange Sorcery* No. 12 (2010).

"Supernatural Refugees," *Star*Line* 33.1 (2010).

"Swamp Fantasy," *Weird Fiction Review* No. 4 (2013).

"Thing of Spring," *Dreams and Nightmares* No. 84 (2009).

"Trans-Neptunian Shores," *Mythic Delirium* No. 25 (2011).

"Valley of the Sorcerers," *Weird Fiction Review* No. 4 (2013).

"A Vessel for Black Waters," *Nameless* No. 2 (2012).

"The Witch of Time," *Nameless* No. 1 (2012).

"The Worm Conjurer," *Mountain Magic: Spellbinding Tales of Appalachia*, ed. Brian J. Hatcher (Woodland Press, 2010).

All other works are original to this collection.

CPSIA information can be obtained at www.ICGtesting.com
Printed in the USA
BVOW04s1620220914

367495BV00005B/16/P

9 781614 981022